SEASONS OF THE CRANES

PETER AND CONNIE ROOP

Walker and Company
New York

We dedicate this book to Mother, who, through sharing her love of birds, continues a family tradition. With her constant encouragement, our words take flight.

The authors thank the following people for their invaluable contributions to this book:

George Archibald and Jim Harris of the International Crane Foundation, Tom Stehn of Arkansas National Wildlife Refuge, Ernie Kuyt of the Canadian Wildlife Service, Mary Anne Bishop of the University of Florida, Steven Langfried, D. R. Blankinship, Ron Renault of the Canadian Wildlife Service, Thomas D. Mangelsen, and David Ellis of the Patuxent Wildlife Research Center.

Photo title page: SID RUCKER

Photo this page: NEBRASKA GAME AND PARKS COMMISSION

First published in the United States of America in 1989
by the Walker Publishing Company, Inc.

Published simultaneously in Canada by Thomas Allen & Son
Canada, Limited, Markham, Ontario

Library of Congress Cataloging in Publication Data

Roop, Peter.
Seasons of the cranes / Peter and Connie Roop.
p. cm.
Summary: Follows a family of whooping cranes through a year, in
a world increasingly hostile to their existence.
ISBN 0-8027-6859-8. ISBN 0-8027-6860-1 (lib. bdg.)
1. Whooping crane—Juvenile literature.   [1. Whooping crane.]
I. Roop, Connie. II. Title.
QL696.G84R66 1989
598'.31—dc19   88-39807
CIP
AC

Printed in Hong Kong

10 9 8 7 6 5 4 3 2 1

Book design by Laurie McBarnette

INTRODUCTION

The Whooping Crane symbolizes survival in a century with unprecedented extinction of species.

A half century ago fewer than 20 Whooping Cranes made their perilous 2,700-mile journey between nesting areas in northern Canada and winter haunts along the coast of Texas. But the Whoopers' tenacity for survival, coupled with the efforts of people to protect the cranes from hunters and habitat destruction, has resulted in the slow increase of this traditional flock to about 150 cranes. There are perhaps 20 birds in the wild in the Rocky Mountains and 54 in captivity. The species now numbers close to 200 birds. The Whoopers will survive.

George Archibald
Director of the International Crane Foundation
Baraboo, Wisconsin

FLYWAY OF THE WHOOPING CRANES

Wood Buffalo National Park

Alberta

Saskatchewan

Montana

N. Dakota

S. Dakota

Nebraska

Kansas

Oklahoma

Texas

Aransas National Wildlife Refuge

Winter is leaving the tundra wetlands of Wood Buffalo National Park in northern Canada. The warming sun melts the last snow of the passing season.

Ripples roll across the water of a shallow pond. The raspy croaks of a lone wood frog announce the wakening day. Butterflies whirl over the wetlands. A rambling bear drinks from the pond. In the distance, the branches of a spruce creak in the wind.

The frog croaks again, but its voice is drowned out

The Whooping Cranes unite in a call. THOMAS D. MANGELSEN/IMAGES OF NATURE®

The cranes in their courtship dance. U.S. FISH AND WILDLIFE SERVICE

by the trumpeting call of a Whooping Crane.

"KER-LEE-OO. KER-LEE-OO."

The call echoes throughout the marsh and nearby woods.

"KER-LEE-OO. KER-LEE-OO."

The large white cranes, their wings tipped in black, swing in a wide spiral out of the clear sky. Two more Whooping Cranes have returned to Wood Buffalo.

The birds, a male and a female, bank and turn

The male watches for predators with his piercing yellow eyes. THOMAS D. MANGELSEN/IMAGES OF NATURE®

gracefully as they approach a possible nesting territory. But they fly on as they see another pair of cranes already established in the pond.

The four birds call back and forth to each other.

The cranes find another nesting site, a pond surrounded by clumps of bulrushes. Fluttering their wings, they glide down and land.

In an age-old instinctive pattern, the newly mated cranes bow their heads and quickly raise them. Beaks pointed at the sky, they unite in their unique call and announce the return to their spring home.

The Whooping Cranes immediately begin stalking the marshy wetlands. After their 2,700-mile journey from Texas, they are anxious to start nest building.

They are also very hungry. The long-legged Whoopers hunt snails and damselflies. As they search for food, they claim a territory of nearly two square miles for their future family.

After feeding, the cranes preen themselves. They dip their beaks into the still-chilly water and carefully rearrange their white, satiny-soft feathers.

The sun hangs low on the horizon and the cranes prepare for the coming night. The howl of a gray wolf cuts through the air. An early evening breeze passes through the marsh, rustling the bulrushes, still brown from winter.

The last rays of the sun silhouette the long-legged cranes. Heads raised, the pair calls again in unison. As the silence of evening settles over the ponds and marshes, the cranes stand close together and sleep.

Morning dawns. Ice has formed on the fringes of the ponds. Diamonds of sunlight flash on the frosty bulrushes. Awake and alert, the cranes call together to the new day.

They feed on snails, leeches, and water bugs, leaving trails of their three-toed tracks on the muddy pond bottom. As they feed, they search for a safe nesting site.

Suddenly, the male crane leaps into the air. He lands, dipping his long neck in front of his mate. He curves his neck back, raising his seven-foot-wide wings skyward. He sweeps his feathers through the air.

"KER-LEE-OO," he calls as he begins another round of the courtship dance.

Two eggs nest in the shallow bulrush bowl. ERNIE KUYT

The female watches her mate as he sways and prances, weaves and bobs for her. Within moments she joins him, matching his movements. Arching her broad wings, she chases him into the pond and quickly follows. Together they point their beaks at the sky and trumpet. Their calls echo over the marsh.

Back on shore, the male crouches, then springs five feet into the air. He lands and bends low. Opening his beak, he grabs mud and reeds, flinging them as he scurries behind his companion. With skill and grace he leaps over her.

As the days pass, the cranes dance more often. Their dancing is interrupted only by feeding and nest building. Each dance strengthens the bond between the new mates, who will remain with each other for life.

As the days lengthen, the courting becomes more intense. The Whoopers eat, preen themselves, dance, rest, and renew their dancing.

Tall bulrushes are trampled, broken, and carried to the nest site. The surrounding bulrushes camouflage the nest. Slowly the cranes build a mound of reeds nearly three feet across. A shallow bowl in the center is left for the eggs.

The first egg is laid. The olive-colored egg, sprinkled with brown spots, is four inches long. The female stays on the nest several hours, scarcely moving. Her mate feeds and preens himself while watching the surrounding marsh. Stretching to his full height of almost five feet, he peers over the tops of the bulrushes, watching for predators with his yellow eyes.

The female cries softly, calling him to relieve her. He walks slowly to the nest, pausing between each two steps. He stops twice, once to peck a freshwater clam and again to look and assure their safety.

The female stands, stretching to her full height. Nearly as tall as her mate, she flaps her wings and steps carefully off the nest.

The male nudges the egg, rolling it over gently with his beak. The female stalks away while the male settles himself on the nest. He twists and turns until the egg rests comfortably beneath him. Feeding and preening, the female takes up the patrol.

A second egg is laid the following morning. The two eggs, twice as long as chicken eggs, lie side by side in the shallow bowl of bulrushes. The cranes continue to exchange duties. With each change the eggs are rolled over so that a healthy chick grows inside.

Late that same day another crane flies over the pond.

"KER-LOO," cries the male, rising from the nest.

"KER-LEE-OO," comes the answering call from the

The female snuggles protectively over the eggs. CANADIAN WILDLIFE SERVICE/ENVIRONMENTAL CANADA®

approaching bird.

The male steps off the nest. The female snuggles protectively over the eggs. Flapping his wide wings, the male moves rapidly away from the nest. He stops when he reaches the edge of their territory.

The incoming crane lands nearby and begins searching for food. The male, angered by the intruder and determined to drive him away, calls again and again.

"KER-LOO, KER-LOO, KER-LOO."

He flaps his huge wings, spreading his jet black wingtips to appear more fearsome.

The intruder continues to feed but makes no effort to challenge the protective crane. He feeds further away from the nest. When his hunger is satisfied, he spreads his wings, rises skyward, and skims over the pond. Without a mate, he will be unable to claim a territory of his own.

The male crane remains on the ground, his red-capped head motionless.

Now that the intruder has left, he begins patrolling the entire boundary of the territory. He circles the pond, stalks to the edge of the spruce trees, crosses the narrow twisting stream. Occasionally he pauses to spear a frog or snatch a dragonfly.

For the next thirty days the watchful cranes keep the eggs warm as the chicks inside grow.

A moose wanders through the pond each morning, feeding on the tender sedge grasses. The cranes watch her closely. Whenever she feeds too near the nest, the cranes trumpet their call of alarm, and the moose moves off in a different direction.

Black bears, wolves, and lynx are rapidly chased away from the cranes' territory. Soaring eagles and swooping great horned owls keep their distance from the ever vigilant cranes, knowing their hard, sharp beaks can cause great pain.

Early one morning the cranes hear a weak peeping sound coming from one of the eggs. The peeping continues all that day and into the next. In the early afternoon a tiny beak pokes a hole through the shell.

The chick taps and chips at the shell all afternoon. Using the eggtooth on the end of its beak, the chick slowly enlarges the hole. By late afternoon the chick

The downy chick is a reddish ball no bigger than an adult robin. U.S. FISH AND WILDLIFE SERVICE

knocks away the last of the shell, sheds its watery membrane, and dives at once under the warm feathers of its mother.

A little later the chick emerges. A warm breeze fluffs her to a reddish ball no bigger than a robin. The newborn crane is so weary from her struggle to hatch that she can stand for only a few minutes.

Night falls. It gets colder, but the mother warms her chick and egg through the night. Standing on guard, the father protects his family.

By morning the crane chick is stronger. She takes several wobbly steps on her shaky legs. The male crane watches the chick while warming the second egg. The female leaves her family, poking and probing for food with her long beak. She eats for herself and then returns to the nest with a grasshopper in her beak. She crushes the grasshopper and dangles the morsel in front of her chick. The chick pecks at the bit of food. The female drops the grasshopper onto the ground, and the peeping chick pecks again. Tilting her head, she swallows the grasshopper bit by bit.

The second egg hatches that afternoon. It is a male. Like his sister, this chick is out of the nest and wobbling about within a day.

The family abandons the nest the next day.

The crane chicks instinctively peck at everything: sticks, rocks, bugs, each other, even their parents' legs. Only occasionally do they succeed in capturing their own food. Both parents bring them dragonflies, damselflies, and grasshoppers to eat.

The female chick, hatched first, is bigger than her brother. Her parents feed her first. She often fights with her brother and steals his food.

As they eat more and more the little cranes grow tremendously fast, sometimes as much as an inch a day.

As the chicks grow taller, the days lengthen. By the time the ruddy sun sets on the last day of spring, the two young cranes stand a foot tall.

Twenty hours of sunlight grace Canada's far northern wilderness that day. Twilight quietly and gently ends the first season of the cranes.

Summer dawns crisp and clear in Wood Buffalo National Park. The young cranes watch as their parents salute the approaching day with a brilliant unison call. They, too, raise their heads to call.

The young cranes continue to imitate their parents. They spread their small wings and flap them. They jab at damselflies and probe the mud for worms. Instinctively, they learn what it is to be a Whooping Crane.

One morning the young female crane wanders

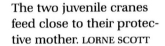

The cranes spend most of their time feeding. ERNIE KUYT

The two juvenile cranes feed close to their protective mother. LORNE SCOTT

alone to the edge of the pond. She pecks at a grasshopper, but misses. The insect springs into the air, landing at the foot of a bulrush. The youngster moves closer. She stabs at it with her short, sharp beak. This time she catches the grasshopper and swallows it.

Still hungry, she probes a tangled mass of tall grass, hoping to find more insects. She startles a wood frog. An instant later the frog escapes into the nearby pond.

Hurrying in pursuit, the young crane trips and falls headfirst into the pond.

She comes up cheeping. She instinctively swims until her three long toes find footing on the muddy bottom.

Her persistent cheeping attracts a parent's attention. Her father stalks through the reeds, brushing aside clumps of bulrushes as he approaches.

By the time he arrives, the dripping youngster has stepped out of the water and is vigorously shaking herself. After preening a few ruffled feathers and peeping with hurt pride, the young crane joins her father.

By midsummer the crane chicks stand over two feet tall. However, as large as they are, they still need the protection of their parents.

The growing cranes become increasingly skillful at spearing dragonflies and damselflies. They easily catch leeches and frogs.

At night the cranes sleep on their feet. Even while asleep, the parents remain vigilant, their senses alert for the slightest danger.

But even their watchfulness isn't enough to stop a hungry, determined predator.

A lynx enters the crane's territory. The lynx watches the feeding cranes. He hasn't eaten for several days and is hungry enough to risk the danger of the cranes with their deadly beaks.

The lynx concentrates on the smaller, chick cranes. Unaware of the danger lurking nearby, the young male crane wanders away from his parents, chasing an insect.

The lynx cautiously follows, keeping hidden in the forest undergrowth. He is wary, knowing the power of a crane's beak.

Suddenly he pounces on the chick, slashing at its throat with penetrating claws. His teeth snap onto the crane's neck. The chick struggles, flapping his wings as the lynx begins pulling him toward the trees.

The commotion instantly alerts the adult cranes and the female immediately plunges after the lynx.

The lynx hears the crane coming and loosens his grip on the young crane. The injured bird drops while the lynx turns to face the approaching female.

Spotting the lynx, the crane bugles. Spreading her wings, she attacks the lynx with her daggerlike beak, jabbing again and again at him. The lynx backs away, looks at his lost prey, and then bounds off into the twilight.

The other two cranes quickly reach the female's side. Together they come close to the injured crane. His eyelids flutter a few times and then close. His body goes limp. He is dead, his jugular vein slashed by the lynx.

The three of them stay with the dead crane for the rest of the evening, whooping occasionally.

As dawn arrives, the parents maintain their watch over their remaining youngster. Every few seconds, one of the pair lifts its red-capped head and looks around to insure their safety. Later in the morning, they return to their roost. The dead young crane remains behind.

Summer passes.

The moose, now with a calf of her own, browses along the edge of the marsh. The calf trails behind its mother, walking stiffly on its long legs.

Hawks circle overhead, waiting to swoop down on unsuspecting prey. Red-winged blackbirds trill from their perches on the bending tips of the bulrushes.

The young crane stands nearly four feet tall. LORNE SCOTT

The marsh hums with whirling dragonflies, swarming mosquitoes, and gnats. Frogs croak constantly.

By the time she is two months old, the crane chick's plumage is a rusty color, turning white near the base of the feathers. She stands nearly four feet tall.

The cranes spend most of their time feeding and resting. The bottoms of the ponds are crisscrossed with crane tracks.

Early one morning, the father crane leans forward into the wind, arching his long neck. He runs, beating his large outstretched wings. Several short, choppy strokes take him airborne. Each stroke carries him higher and higher over the marsh.

Climbing into the sky, circling, gliding on beautiful white, black-tipped wings, he turns his head from side to side, regal in his passing.

He banks to his left as a fox enters their territory. His alarm call crosses the wetlands. Dipping his wings, he plunges from the sky toward the invader.

Far below, his mate takes action immediately. Calling to the young female, she leads her into the relative safety of the deeper marsh water.

Startled by the sharp bugling of the diving male crane, the fox quickly retreats. He stops at the forest edge to survey the source of the commotion. Seeing the huge male dropping toward him, the fox turns tail and disappears into the woods.

The two adult cranes become restless. They take to the air more often now.

The young crane imitates her parents. She leans into the wind, arches her neck, runs, and usually stumbles and falls.

Early one morning the female crane takes off. Her youngster imitates her, running toward the water. She flaps her broad wings rhythmically. She matches her steps with the beat of her wings. She pushes down hard as she runs and a gust of wind pushes behind her.

Suddenly she is off the ground. Her wings beat several more times and she stays aloft for nearly fifty yards.

She has flown. She is a fledgling now.

Later that day she makes another short flight.

Within a week she flies across the pond with her father, just skimming the surface as she takes off.

The fledgling chick learns that taking off is easier than landing. Coming in for a landing, the inexperienced chick misjudges her speed. She lands too close to a lightning-split spruce and her momentum carries her into the jagged stump.

Crashing to the ground, she lays stunned. Her satiny white feathers turn red as blood trickles from her wounds. Panting, she waits for her parents to join her.

The young crane soon recovers her breath. The bleeding stops. Struggling to her feet, she stands. With her parents cheeping at her side, the youngster takes a few halting steps and begins walking slowly across the marsh.

Gradually the young bird gains confidence as she masters the art of safe landings.

The weather begins to change. The nights are cooler and the days are shorter. Food becomes scarce. Frost fringes the plants and thin ice rings the ponds in the early morning hours.

After a summer of protecting and caring for their young crane, the adults fly more often. They need to exercise their wings to regain the strength needed to migrate thousands of miles to their winter home in Texas.

With short, rhythmic strokes of their long wings, the three cranes cut swiftly across the blue sky. They fly in formation with the male and female adult exchanging the lead position as they seek out feeding areas further and further from their familiar marsh territory. The young crane works hard to keep pace.

On their feeding grounds, they eat ravenously for

nearly ten hours, gradually building up the fat needed for the long migration. Overhead geese, ducks, and other migratory birds are heard as they travel to southern wintering grounds.

The hazy sun tracks lower and lower across the remote Canadian sky. The day draws to a close as the cranes return to their roosting area. When they land, it is clear that the young crane is nearly as tall as her parents. The three birds settle for the night.

Each morning more and more of the pond is frozen. Although many of the park's summer birds have flown to warmer climates, the cranes continue to prepare themselves.

Finally the first fat, wet snowflakes fall. Ice makes it increasingly difficult to catch food in the ponds. The cold has killed most of their favorite insects.

The time to migrate has arrived.

The cranes feed one last time. Mid-morning on a clear, frosty October day, they spiral upward. As if to say goodbye, they call loudly as they circle the marsh one more time before turning south.

The cranes slowly fade in the distance, their calls echoing through the wilderness. The cranes are on the wing again, following an ancient, timeless path to warmer days and more plentiful food.

The Whooping Crane summer is over.

18

Flying a mile high, the three cranes pass over the broad golden wheat fields and scattered villages of Saskatchewan.

The cranes begin to glide down in wide spirals. Their ride on the hot rising air of the thermal is over as this air cools. Each turn brings them closer to the sun-warmed earth. They adjust their glide to bring them to a small lake.

The autumn sky is speckled with thousands of birds migrating on the same flyway that the cranes

The three cranes land in a nearby wheat field.
THOMAS D. MANGELSEN/IMAGES OF NATURE®

The three cranes feed until dark. LORNE SCOTT

follow. Great groups of geese pass, honking as they arrow through the chilly air. Flocks of ducks angle southward. Single songbirds wing their way to a gentler climate.

The cranes fly over 180 miles that first day of migration. The family occasionally spirals down to rest and feed. Now they stop early in the afternoon because the young crane is tired.

The crane family spends its first night of the long migration on the shore of a lake. The birds eat until

19

The cranes take to the air again. LORNE SCOTT

the sky grows dark. Weary from their arduous flight, the young crane and her parents sleep.

In the morning, after feeding, the three cranes take to the air again.

Each day the young crane flies further. The crane family now covers three hundred miles from dawn to sunset. At night, they glide down to a marsh, a beaver pool, or a riverbank, where they feed and sleep.

One afternoon the cranes land beyond a patch of

reeds. They stalk along the riverbank, hunting for insects and small fish. Finding little to satisfy them, they fly to a nearby wheat field.

They peck at grain dropped by the harvesting machines. They hunt crickets and grubs in the stubble. Food is so plentiful that they stay to rest and feed for several days. The parents occasionally dance as if to celebrate the feast.

The next day a different group of Whoopers spirals down to feed in the same fields. Two cranes stand guard while the other cranes feed. When all the cranes have eaten, they take to the air again to continue their migration.

Two days later the parents and their young crane rise to the sky again.

Late one November afternoon, after entering the United States, the cranes cross the wide Missouri River. They fly low over the muddy water, searching for a place to rest for the night.

The following day at sunset the cranes see the Platte River meandering over the rolling prairie, cutting broad curves into the earth. Dozens of islands and sandbars offer safe roosting spots for them as well as their cousins, the Sandhill Cranes.

The three Whooping Cranes rest and feed on a sandbar in the middle of the river. At times they wade in the shallows, snatching minnows and crayfish. Occasionally they fly to nearby cornfields to peck for scattered ears of corn. They feast on earthworms.

Early one morning the cranes are startled by gunfire near their roost. They whoop excitedly and prepare to fly. The shooting stops, but the birds settle down only after it has been quiet for a long time.

The gunfire comes again, this time much closer to

the cranes. The young crane is bewildered by the loud noises. Her parents, however, are familiar with the danger of men and guns. The father crane whoops and takes off. The fledgling follows, with her mother lifting off behind her. They leave the Platte.

The cranes continue their migration. They fly over farms, towns, cities, and highways. They spiral down to feed and take to the air again. Sometimes they stay in one place for a week to rest and to eat their fill.

The parents dance as they make their way south.
THOMAS D. MANGELSEN/IMAGES OF NATURE®

Late one afternoon they land in a field to hunt for food. High-tension electrical lines stretch along the edge of the field. The cranes land far away from the wires. They can see a twisted patch of white caught high in the lines. Even from a distance they can tell that a crane got tangled in the wires and died. The adult cranes have seen such accidents before.

A month later, the cranes reach the broad salt marshes of the Texas coast. They make a wide sweep over the indented coast, searching for a protected cove or inlet to stake their territory.

Suddenly the male calls urgently. Below them stretches a meadow of rippling marsh grass edged on one side by upland shrubs and oaks. The other side of the meadow slants down to a shallow tidal stream that leads to a cove of calm water. Seeing no other cranes in this territory, they make one final circle and land in the cove.

It is high tide. The adult cranes easily capture several blue crabs, one of their favorite winter foods. The young crane begs a crab from her mother and then eagerly hunts more for herself.

After feeding, the cranes crisscross the cove on foot, claiming this territory for themselves. No other crane raises a call of protest as they stalk the entire boundary of their four-hundred-acre territory. The young crane follows her parents, learning the borders of her new home. Still hungry even after five crabs, she snaps grasshoppers and pecks snails along the way.

The cranes settle for the night on the shore of the cove. Calling in unison, the adults announce their return to the Aransas National Wildlife Refuge as the autumn season of the cranes ends.

A light fog brought by a wind settles over the salt marsh. Flocks of sandpipers scurry by as pintail ducks pass overhead in the cool, ghostly air. By midday the sun burns the fog away.

The cranes hear the high-pitched bugles of another family of Whoopers. The new crane family circles and lands in the cove.

The female stands upright, alerted to the invaders. She issues a challenging call. "KER-LOO." The intruding Whoopers together emit a shrill reply.

The male patrols the boundaries of their territory. U.S. FISH AND WILDLIFE SERVICE

Two cranes take to the air after being chased by the defending male. JEFF FOOTT

With three to feed, the cranes are determined to secure a bountiful territory for themselves.

The male, responding to his mate's urgent calls, flies to her aid. Together they face the challenging family.

The male crane extends his neck and struts around. He arches his neck and trumpets. He spreads his broad wings, flapping them furiously. Standing at his full height, he charges at his enemies.

The invading cranes respond, arching their necks and flapping their wings.

The calls of the competing cranes can be heard for miles. Cry follows cry as the cranes fight for the territory.

Finally the three intruding cranes concede. Tired and hungry from their recent flight, they give in to the rested and well-fed crane family. A last piercing whoop and charge from the defending male sends them on their way to search for an unchallenged territory.

The cranes return to feeding after the intruders flee. The young crane stays within a few yards of her mother, begging for food.

The female catches a small blue crab. Calling, "pseep, pseep," the fledgling begs her mother to share the small crab. After breaking off the claws, she gives the crab to her youngster. The ever-hungry crane gulps the crab down while her mother swallows the claws.

Still on the alert, the adult male watches and listens, stalking the boundaries of their territory. Only when he is assured that the danger has passed does he resume feeding.

In mid-January a deadly calm settles over the Texas coast. The ponds, normally shimmering with gentle waves, are still. Songbirds stop chirping in the upland shrubs. Insects stop whirring. The Whooping Cranes retreat to the uplands of their territory.

They seek refuge in the brush hugging the ground, their long legs folded beneath them. Overhead, thunderclouds build in tall, dark towers.

Suddenly, a strong, warm wind rips through the salt marsh. Grasses and rushes bend to the ground under the assault of the wind. Booming waves crash against the shore.

The young crane, unfamiliar with such a fierce thunderstorm, stands up. At once the wind sweeps the inexperienced bird off her feet. Frightened and calling frantically, the fledgling tries to regain her balance. The wind tumbles her over again and carries her cries away from her parents.

Each time she stands, she is swept over again. Finally, she gives in to the wind and huddles on the

The male crane rushes to aid his mate in defending their territory. SID RUCKER

ground, folding her wings tightly for protection.

The steel-gray cloud cover slowly moves east. The sun reappears and the young crane rejoins her parents. Wet and bedraggled, she stands near them for comfort.

By early March the fledged chick has grown less dependent on her parents. She often wanders alone to feed, snatching snails off the cordgrass and spearing her own crabs.

Throughout the salt marsh, unison calls are heard

as old bonds are strengthened and new bonds made. The adult male and female cranes begin dancing more often in preparation for mating.

Warm spring winds signal winter's end and as winter leaves Aransas, so do the cranes.

One morning the male arches his neck and bugles loudly. The three cranes rise with the sun, spiraling higher and higher on the warm updrafts. They call to each other and to the world.

The beautiful, rare Whooping Cranes begin the

The three cranes glide over the salt marsh. D. R. BLANKINSHIP

long return journey to their spring home in Canada.

The young crane, almost a year old now, will journey to Wood Buffalo with her parents. There, she will leave her parents to join other young cranes.

In four more years she will find a mate. These two cranes will dance, unite in their call, and remain together for life. Like their ancestors for millions of years, they will mate, and raise their own chicks.

The Whooping Cranes will continue to survive the seasons.

11/29/90